The Little Bear That Could

One Rescue Pup's Journey of Healing

By Ku

Kuruk: The Little Bear That Could

Copyright © 2013 by Julianne Victoria and Through the Peacock's Eyes Press

All rights reserved. This book may not be reproduced in whole or part, stored in retrieval system or transmitted in any form or by any means – electronic, mechanical, or other – without written permission from the publisher, except by a reviewer, who may quote brief passages in a review.

www.peacockseyes.com

Overcoming fear
And learning to trust humans
Lessons taught by Love

Introduction

Kuruk Babybear
Malamute from Alaska
All pups need is Love

Hellooowooowooo! Welcome to my book! I am going to tell you the story of my rescue and my healing journey. I've travelled over 3,000 miles, but Mama says I've come light-years! I'm not sure how far that is, but it sure sounds like it is much farther than 3,000 miles. I think it's her way of telling others how proud she is of me, but really I am very proud of Mama. Without her I don't think I would be where I am today.

What did she do, you ask? She showered me with love! Everyone deserves to be loved, and that is why I have decided to tell my story: to inspire other humans to help rescue pups, kitties, or other animals, to bring courage to all the rescue animals who are still healing, and to raise money through book sales to donate and help out animal rescue groups.

Besides this book, I also am the poetic pup behind the blog Haiku By Ku, www.haikubyku.com. I have always thought thoughts in haiku. I don't know why. Maybe I was a Japanese Akita in a past life, but in this life I am an Alaskan Malamute. I will include several haiku in this book as well.

On my blog's About Page, you will find links to the newspaper article about my rescue, as well as a video about my journey from Alaska to Seattle. Thank you for your interest in my story and in animal rescue. Wooooowooooo!

p.s. Most snow pups never, or rarely, bark. We sing! Wooooowooooo!

Alaska

I lived on a chain

Born into captivity

Humans with hearts came

I was born in the great outdoors near a town called Wasilla in Alaska to my pack of 170 Alaskan Malamutes. We are genetically very close to wolves and we even look a lot like wolves, but we are a very mellow and sweet breed of dog. We like to be with humans: working and pulling sleds, running, hiking, playing, and even just lounging around. But my pup pack in Alaska didn't get to be with humans because we lived in a place called a puppy mill.

I vaguely remember when I was a very, very little baby pup romping around and playing with my siblings. Mostly, however, I remember being stuck on a four-foot chain like the rest of my pack family. Mamapup tried her best to teach us and keep us entertained, but most days were filled with boredom. We wanted to run and wrestle and go on adventures.

We tried to make the best of the situation, and my siblings and I learned to play and wrestle on our chains without getting all tangled up. I must have learned well, because my Mama now says I am like Houdini (whoever that is), and can get myself untangled no matter how twisted and tied I might get my leash.

To help with some of the boredom, the grandparent pups would tell us kids amazing stories about pups who got to go on adventures. One of them was about a race for snow pups called the Iditarod! Oh how I dreamt of being able to run and run free as a wolf!

They told us other wonderful stories too about how there were pups all over the world who live with humans and other animals in dry and cozy homes where they get food, water, and cuddling every day. The grandparents even told us about treats. I wasn't really sure what that was, but it sounded awesome!

My first year of life was rough. Besides being stuck on a chain, we often didn't have enough food and water. Sometimes we went days with nothing to live off of but snow and a little dirt, and it only got worse. When I was about one year old, some of our pack members started to die. It was very traumatic and sad to see my family members pass away before my eyes.

And then one day when we had eaten all the snow that we could reach and all seemed hopeless, some humans suddenly came and put all of us into crates. They loaded us onto big trucks and took us all away. I was terrified! I had no idea what was going on. Being in a crate was even worse than the chain. At least on the chain I could move a little.

These strange humans took us all to a place called a shelter where other humans called vets looked at us and poked us. Some of my pack were too weak from hunger and dehydration to resist, but I sure tried. I had never been touched by a human before, and this didn't seem like the cuddling the grandparent pups had told us about.

Despite the humans, living at the shelter was much better than the puppy mill. We had plenty of fresh water and food, and we could move around and play in the cages. I was with my cousins, but sadly I was separated from my Mamapup and siblings. I started to accept that this was what my life was to be and that I could do it, but after the third full moon everything changed again.

The Big Bird

Up high in the sky
Flying over the mountains
My journey began

The crates appeared again. This time, though, the humans only took four of us. We were in these crates for a long time: first on a truck, then in a place called an airport, and then on an airplane. I had seen these airplanes way up in the sky before. I thought that they were big noisy birds, but now I knew that they're flying machines. It sure was extra noisy inside it, and that did not help my anxiety! I think I shook the whole flight.

After what seemed like a very long time and a big thud, we were taken out of the airplane's belly and into another airport. Then we were taken out of the crates to stretch our legs. Whewwooo! Just in time because I really needed to go potty!

Four nice ladies then loaded us into other trucks and took us to another shelter. When we got there, we walked around outside for a little bit. The four of us were: wise Uncle Kävik, me, a distant cousin, and my brother Loki. Loki was very wary of everything and would howl and cry out in fear. I was extremely shy, but quiet. The nice ladies gave us our first treats to help us feel better. It worked for Loki, but not for me. I was too unsure about what was going on and would stay as far on the leash as possible.

I learned that these humans were part of a rescue group called the Washington Alaskan Malamute Adoption League (WAMAL). They seemed to be in tune with us pups and were able to pick up on our names intuitively. Even though I was very, very shy they could see the deep introspective wisdom of the bear in my eyes, and named me "Kuruk," which means "bear" in the Native American Pawnee language.

I had to draw upon the wisdom of my inner bear to help me each and every day. Every day there were new things that caused me great fear, so I had to keep telling myself I could do it. We all stayed at the shelter together for a couple of weeks until different humans started to take each of us away one by one.

Foster Mama Miss Cindy

Dear Miss Cindy K
The bestest foster Mama
Ice cream is yummy

After the next full moon, a foster Mama named Miss Cindy came and took me away from the shelter. I was sad, scared, anxious, curious, and terrified! What was a foster Mama? She had two other pups with her so she must be ok, I figured. There was a very pretty Siberian Husky named Tara and a Malamute-Husky named Timber. Timber was a little protective of his sister Tara, but I knew he was just full of grumbles.

Right away we drove into the mountains to hike on some trails. I'd never gone for a hike, nor had I ever walked so far on a leash! I paced and paced and paced whether we were moving or not. I stayed as far away from everyone as I could so I could observe all that was going on. My eyes were big as saucers and my heart was pounding as hard as the airplane thud.

Miss Cindy took me to her home after the hike. I was to live with her and Tara and Timber until they found me a forever home. Was it really true? Was I going to live in a home like the grandparents told us? Miss Cindy's home was nice. We had a big room to play in and a big yard to run around in.

After a few weeks I started to get used to a house and didn't have to be lured inside with food as much, but my anxiety was still there. The vets in Alaska had put me on medicine for it. Miss Cindy had started to cut down on the dose, but it would still be a long time until I did not feel scared and unsure all the time. I just kept telling myself that I could do it!

My Shining Star

Beautiful Tara
Siberian Husky girl
She gave me courage

Foster Mama Cindy took all of us pups on lots of hikes. Sometimes other humans and big Malamutes joined us too. It really helped me to observe the other pups interacting with their humans, but what really helped me the most was Tara. She was my shining star. She asked her Mama Cindy to leash me to her so she could teach me how to travel as a pack. She also showed me how to approach humans and ask for treats! I really liked these treat things, so I learned fast.

Tara and I bonded, and you could even say we fell in love. Without her love and encouragement I might not have had such a good start to my healing journey. She kept telling me that I could do it, and I believed her. I could do it!

Tara had a rough start to life too. When she was just a baby, she broke one of her legs. Her humans decided they did not love her and abandoned her in her time of greatest need. Luckily the Washington Alaskan Malamute Adoption League (WAMAL) that Miss Cindy fosters for took her in and treated her broken leg. Tara was only supposed to be with Miss Cindy as a foster pup, but she ended up as a foster failure instead. Wooooowooooo! Miss Cindy became Tara's forever Mama.

The Strange Visitors

They came together
A lady and big Simba
Just strangers to me

I had been living with Miss Cindy for just one moon cycle when one day a pretty lady with a very big Malamute named Simba came to visit me. Simba took me out to the backyard to talk to me and get to know me. He had lived with Miss Cindy when he was a foster pup too, so he knew the place well. He tried to get me to go say hi to this strange lady, but I would not get close. Then Miss Cindy lured me with food and we all went inside to talk.

Inside the pretty lady looked into my eyes and spoke to me. She did not use words though. She knew how to talk with her eyes! Then the mighty Simba came over next to her, and she asked him if he thought I could be his little brother. What?! I was so excited and scared at the same time! Was I really going to have my own home and family?!

Before they left, Simba and Miss Cindy did some catching up. He told her that he would be a good big brother and help his Mama teach me everything. A Mama?! Was I really going to have my own Mama?! They then asked me if I would like to live with them. I was very nervous and shy, but I said: ok.

This was what I had always wanted. I was so scared, but knew I could do it! A week later my new Mama came back. She put a new purple collar and harness on me, and gave me a hug and kiss. She took me to her car, and off we went.

My Own Home

She took me away
To a place called my own home
Home sweet home indeed

The car ride only took a few minutes. My new Mama talked to me the whole way. She said that Simba was home waiting for me, and that I would also have two kitty siblings and chickens. I had seen kitties at Miss Cindy's house, but I did not know what chickens were. Mama said they were kind of like ducks, which I had seen before in Alaska.

When we arrived...pup, oh, pup...it was true! It was true! The stories the grandparent pups had told us kids were true! I had my very own home! It was cozy and dry with other animals, water, food, and big yard to run free in.

My new Mama was very sweet and patient with me, especially when I'd refuse to come in from the yard. She took me and big brother Simba on walks twice a day. She also took me on short runs, which helped me to burn off some anxious energy.

I had to learn so much! Simba was very helpful. He taught me everything he knew, which made things easy for Mama. Mama poured all her love into me too. It wasn't long before I didn't jump at cars driving by and have panic attacks when humans wanted to come near me. Teenagers were especially frightening, but the vet said he thought they were too! Even though there was so much to absorb and so much anxiety to overcome, I knew I could do it.

I needed lots of healing, but I was confident I could do that too. It took nearly six months of lots of patience from Mama, but over that time I got off the anxiety medicine, had gained a total of 50 pounds since my time in Alaska, stopped pacing most of time, and slowly got used to humans.

Simba

The mighty Simba
All one hundred forty pounds
A true lion king

Big brother Simba was big and mighty. Mama says he was a very old soul. I couldn't have asked for a better big brother to teach me. And I learned quickly! Simba taught me everything so well, Mama never had to do a single training session with me.

Simba had an even rougher start to life than I did. I had known nothing else but life at the puppy mill. Simba had had a happy home at the start when he was a puppy, but when he was about two he was abandoned on a chain by his mom. He and his Husky sister were tied up and left in the backyard for four years! Eventually, a neighbor took in the Husky and a relative took Simba.

Simba had so many physical and emotional pains. He had been neglected, barely fed or given water, and was so lacking in exercise that he was hardly able to use his hind legs. After being rescued he had to be shaved to remove the parasites in his fur, and he had other skin and health issues. Worst of all, he had chewed on his infected paws so severely that the vets had at first thought he had chewed his toes off.

The kind relative had many pets of her own, and wanted to get Simba healthy enough to surrender him to a rescue group for adoption. It was through WAMAL that Mama found him. She says it was love at first sight when she saw his picture on the website. Simba said that too because when Mama went to Miss Cindy's to meet him, he took one look at her and said: Iwuvyooowoooowooooo!

Mama had poured all her love and healing energy-work into Simba for two years by the time I joined the pack, but you would never have known the sadness and pain that had filled Simba's past. He was the gentlest giant, wise and kind. His paws were mostly healed, his skin problems were gone, and his fur had all grown back. Simba's lion-heart courage gave me even more courage that I could do it too!

Sadly the mighty Simba passed away two months after becoming my brother, but he is forever in our hearts.

A Sister

My sister Nalle

Mama calls her goofy girl

Perfect eyeliner

It was on New Year's Day 2012, when I had been with Mama and my pack for about six months, that I composed my first haiku for Mama. It's the very first one in the Introduction to this book. My confidence was growing and I was not afraid to express myself anymore. I had peeled off many layers of worry and fear. I still needed healing, but I knew I could do it.

Mama had been very busy working with me to overcome my anxiety, and even though I had adjusted very well to being an only pup, she could see that I needed someone to wrestle and play with regularly. My kitty siblings, Apollo and Zoe, and the chickens did not seem to want to wrestle with me.

So Mama looked and looked to find a good match for our pack, but she did not find the right pup. Finally she emailed WAMAL and let them know she was looking for a sibling for me who was familiar with kitties. (Some Mals who don't know kitties, might mistake them for squirrels.) The next day, they emailed back and told Mama that they found me a sister! Woooooowoooooo! Mama said she was a gift. Nalle didn't come from a bad situation. She just needed a new home.

My sister and I hit it off immediately! Her name is Nalle, which also means "bear," and she is just a little younger than me. We wrestle, and play, and wrestle, and run, and wrestle-wrestle together. Nalle is not shy at all, so she helps me even today when I'm having some shy moments. She reminds me that I can do it.

Nalle is a very pretty Malamute. She has perfect eyeliner and long elegant legs. She loves, loves, loves tummy rubs, and is never shy to ask anyone or any stranger anywhere for a tummy rub. She's my goofy sister and my best friend.

The Journey Continues

Three thousand miles
I have travelled home to home
Journey for new life

It was only a few months after Nalle joined our pack that Mama decided we were going to move back to her hometown of San Francisco. There was lots of packing stuff into boxes and lots of cleaning first, but then we all loaded up in the car (not the chickens though; they found a new home) and took off.

We drove for two days, but it was lots of fun because I love riding in the car! Sometimes Nalle would hog the back seat just like she hogs the toys, but luckily Mals are very good at curling up into little balls to sleep.

Living in this big city is lots of fun. It is very hilly, so it's like we are hiking mountains on every walk. And it's super windy! I love walking into the blustery wind. We meet lots of people here who sometimes give us treats. Sometimes I am still a little shy around strangers, but I am much more comfortable around them. I will usually say hello before Nalle butts in and asks for a tummy rub. Wooo!

My healing journey will continue on, but I know I can do it! And if I can do it, I know other rescue pups, and kitties, and horses, and other animals can do it too!

Wooooooowooooooo!

My Transformation Haiku

Terrified, abused

But lots of love helped me heal

Now a happy pup

My Rescue Poem From A to Z

Alaskan outdoors wild and free
Born was I to a big family
Cold and harsh the weather
Dark the days half the year
Everyone had wooly coats
Freeze though we don't
Grateful for the snow
Happy to nap in its glow
Inuits taught our ancestors well
Justly with humans we wish to dwell
Knowing our intelligence
Like to work at any chance
Many of us began to starve
No one fed us so snow we carved
Only if we could break the chains
Perhaps we'd run free again
Quiet and death lurked in the air
Rescue humans came for us with care
Sadness and love they felt for me
Today I am happy and free

Under lots of care and love

Victoriously I've overcome

Worry, fear, and anxiety

Exceptional my Mama's love for me

Yes, now my new family:

Zoe, Apollo, and Nalle

Acknowledgements

Eternal thanks to the Matanuska-Susitna Borough animal shelter in Alaska, WAMAL in the Seattle, Washington area, Miss Cindy, Tara, Timber, the whole hiking pack, and all those who send love and healing energy, who donate and support, and who rescue, foster, and adopt animals in need. I'd also like to thank the man at the puppy mill. Why you ask? Because he, too, needs love, and without my start to life there, I would not have found my Mama, nor would I be where I am today: able to help other animals like me!

Humans suffer too

Rescue them with compassion

Thank you Alaska!

Made in the USA
San Bernardino, CA
30 September 2013